Columbus Day

ABDO
Publishing Company

A Buddy Book
by
Julie Murray

Visit us at
www.abdopub.com

Published by ABDO Publishing Company, 4940 Viking Drive, Edina, Minnesota 55435.

Copyright © 2005 by Abdo Consulting Group, Inc. International copyrights reserved in all countries. No part of this book may be reproduced in any form without written permission from the publisher. Buddy Books™ is a trademark and logo of ABDO Publishing Company.

Printed in the United States.

Edited by: Sarah Tieck
Contributing Editor: Michael P. Goecke
Graphic Design: Denise Esner
Image Research: Deborah Coldiron, Maria Hosley
Photographs: North Wind Archives, Photodisc, Thinkstock

Library of Congress Cataloging-in-Publication Data

Murray, Julie, 1969-
  Columbus Day / Julie Murray.
      p. cm. — (Holidays)
  Includes bibliographical references and index.
  Contents: Columbus Day — A young Christopher Columbus — Having a dream — The first voyage — New discoveries — Leaving the islands — Welcome home — More trips to the new land — A national holiday.
  ISBN 1-59197-587-5
    1. Columbus Day—Juvenile literature. 2. Columbus, Christopher—Juvenile literature. 3. America—Discovery and exploration—Spanish—Juvenile literature. [1. Columbus Day. 2. Holidays. 3. Columbus, Christopher. 4. America—Discovery and exploration—Spanish.] I. Title.

E120.M87 2004
394.264—dc22

2003063008

Table of Contents

What Is Columbus Day?

Columbus Day celebrates a man's adventures and discoveries. Christopher Columbus was a famous **explorer** who lived about 500 years ago. He helped discover the land that is now called North America and South America.

Christopher Columbus sailed with three ships. They were named the Niña, the Pinta, and the Santa María.

Columbus Day is a national **holiday** in the United States. It is celebrated on the second Monday in October each year. This is the time of year when Christopher Columbus first landed in the New World.

Sailing The Ocean Blue

Christopher Columbus was born in Italy. He lived in Europe in the 1400s. Spain, England, and Italy are some countries in Europe.

Many people dreamed of getting gold, jewels, and spices in the Indies. The Indies are part of Asia. Many sailors in Europe tried to reach Asia by sailing south around Africa. This **route** was long and dangerous.

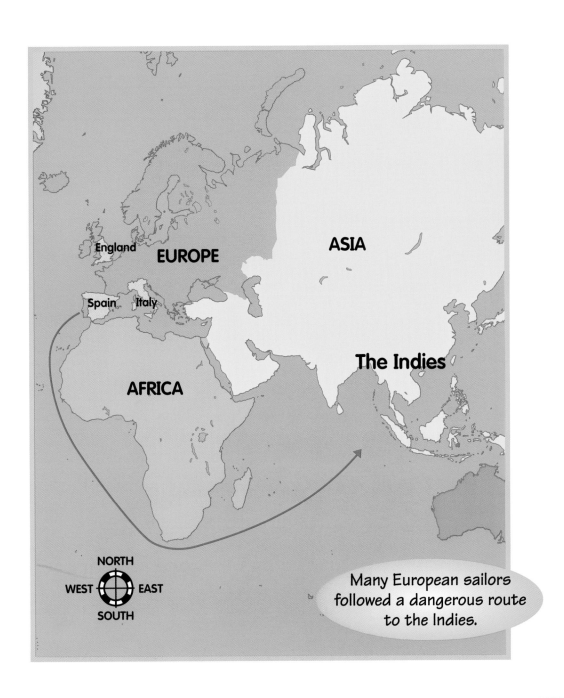

England

EUROPE

Spain   Italy

ASIA

AFRICA

The Indies

NORTH
WEST — EAST
SOUTH

Many European sailors
followed a dangerous route
to the Indies.

Christopher Columbus was an **explorer**. He wanted to find a shorter and safer way to get to Asia.

Christopher Columbus studied maps in Spain.

Discovering
A New World

After studying maps and charts, Christopher Columbus had an idea. He thought sailing west to Asia would be an easier **route**. Many people did not believe him. Still, Christopher Columbus wanted to try.

Christopher Columbus told King Ferdinand and Queen Isabella his ideas.

Christopher Columbus needed money for his trip. In 1492, King Ferdinand and Queen Isabella of Spain gave him the money. He sailed across the Atlantic Ocean to find a new **route**.

He failed at that mission. Instead, he found another land. This land is now called North America and South America.

Not The First To Arrive

Christopher Columbus was not the first person to find the Americas. About 500 years earlier, Scandinavian **explorers** known as Vikings had landed in North America. They did not stay long on the new land.

Vikings sailed to America 500 years before Christopher Columbus.

Christopher Columbus helped connect Europe and the Americas. He made **settlements** in the Americas. He also discovered many other places in his travels.

Columbus Day

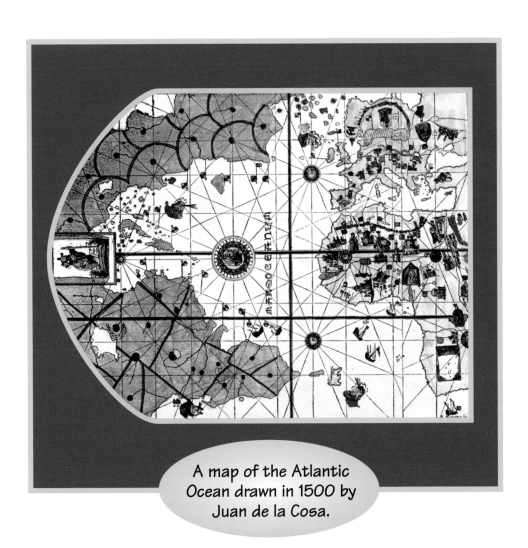

A map of the Atlantic
Ocean drawn in 1500 by
Juan de la Cosa.

The Making Of A Holiday

The first known celebration of Christopher Columbus took place on October 12, 1792, in New York City. On that day, a ceremony honored the 300th anniversary of Christopher Columbus's landing. On October 12, 1866, Italian Americans in New York held the first celebration of the discovery of America.

A Christopher Columbus statue in Barcelona, Spain.

In 1892, people celebrated the 400th anniversary of Christopher Columbus's landing. President Benjamin Harrison made a **proclamation** about the celebration.

The First Columbus Day

Colorado was the first state to celebrate Columbus Day. This happened in 1905.

In 1920, people started celebrating Columbus Day every year. Some states held Columbus Day celebrations each year on October 12. In 1937, President Franklin Delano Roosevelt said Columbus Day was every October 12.

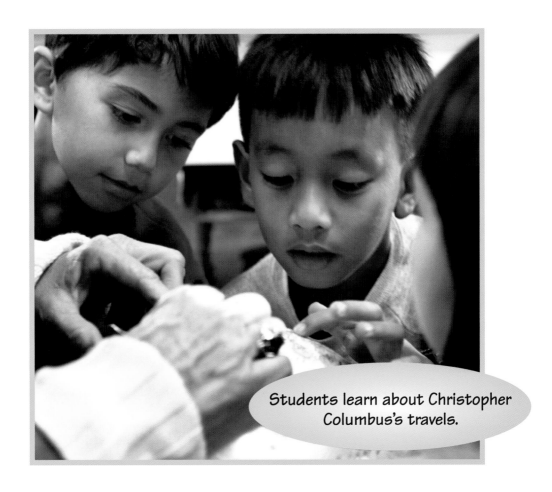

Students learn about Christopher Columbus's travels.

In 1971, Congress made Columbus Day a federal **holiday**. They said it would be celebrated on the second Monday of October every year.

Celebrations Today

Today, people around the United States celebrate Columbus Day. School children study Christopher Columbus's life or watch TV programs about his discoveries. Many cities have parades and celebrations. Government offices, post offices, and some schools and businesses are closed on this holiday.

Important Words

crew a group of people who work together on a ship.

explorer a person who travels to new, or unknown places.

holiday a special time for celebration.

proclamation a public announcement.

route a road or course that has been traveled, or will be traveled.

settlement a small village.

voyage a journey.

Web Sites

To learn more about Columbus Day,
visit ABDO Publishing Company on the World Wide Web. Web site links about Columbus Day are featured on our Book Links page. These links are routinely monitored and updated to provide the most current information available.

www.abdopub.com

Life Of An Explorer

1451—Christopher Columbus was born.

1484—Christopher Columbus asked King John of Portugal to pay for a trip to the Indies. King John said no.

1492—King Ferdinand and Queen Isabella of Spain gave Christopher Columbus money for his trip.

August 3, 1492—Christopher Columbus and his **crew** set sail across the Atlantic Ocean.

October 12, 1492—Christopher Columbus and his crew reached land. They discovered the New World.

October 28, 1492—Christopher Columbus discovered Cuba.

December 5, 1492—Christopher Columbus discovered Hispaniola.

September 1493—Christopher Columbus began a second **voyage** to the New World.

May 30, 1498—Christopher Columbus began a third voyage with six ships.

Summer 1498—Christopher Columbus found South America.

May 11, 1502—Christopher Columbus began his last voyage to the New World.

1506—Christopher Columbus died.

Index